t3

New and Selected Poems

ANNE RIDLER

*New and
Selected Poems*

faber and faber

LONDON · BOSTON

First published in 1988
by Faber and Faber Limited
3 Queen Square London WC1N 3AU

Photoset by Wilmaset Birkenhead Wirral
Printed in Great Britain by
Richard Clay Ltd Bungay Suffolk
All rights reserved

British Library Cataloguing in Publication Data

Ridler, Anne
New and selected poems.
I. Title
821'.912   PR6035.I54

ISBN 0–571–15193–0
ISBN 0–571–15140–X Pbk

Contents

from *A Matter of Life and Death* (1959)

from *Some Time After* (1972)

New Poems

Acknowledgements

Acknowledgements are due to the editors of the following publications, in which some of these previously uncollected poems first appeared: *The Critical Quarterly, The Listener, Only Poetry, Other Poetry, Outposts, PN Review, Temenos, The Yale Magazine.* Also to the publishers of these anthologies: *Between Comets, Cathedrals, Night Ride and Sunrise, People, Ten Oxford Poets.*

from *Poems* (1939)

In Cornwall

Westward where the cliff falls
In dark walls through Cornish seas still haunted
By drowned men who shoulder toward the land,
By grim mermaids and the pained cry of gulls,

I have seen, on fine days
Lying lazy, when all this seemed innocent
(And while I watched, the lemon-coloured tide,
That wrinkles like a melting jelly, rose

To the full mark on sunburnt rock),
I have seen the flicker of light far out on bayonets –
Winking above the wave – of a submerged army
That waits its time. But a cloud sweeps them back

Into an endless milky sea
That seems the bright and easy floor of heaven:
Like heaven that will not let the earth remain
In sin, but grinds its outworks endlessly,

And steals up its shore
With power hidden in the surf's feeling finger.
There saints like ships can navigate, and fair
The crops of golden plants like sparkles shine.
And O that we were there.

Young Man's Song

(from a dramatic fragment)

As white is she
And to my touch as choice and briefly satisfactory
As whitebeam leaves that the wind whips aloft,
That tell to the eye their texture soft:
Sweet message sent
To fingertips, and sweetness quickly spent.

Where she goes
Sliding curtains of the rain on rods of sun her ways
  enclose,
River-whirling gulls her gay sky receives,
Roads, their hostile posters furled,
Bless with arching eaves;
She my love by London gentled as by space the spinning
  world.

from *The Nine Bright Shiners* (1943)

Kirkwall 1942

Far again, far,
And the Pentland howling psalms of separation
Lifts and falls, lifts and falls between.
But present pain
Folds like a firth round islets that contain
A sheepfold and a single habitation –
Moments in our summer of success –
Or the greater islands, colonized and built with peace.

Cold knives of light
Make every outline clear in a northern island,
The separating light, the sea's green;
Yet southern lives
Merge in the lupin fields or sleepy coves,
In crowstepped gables find a hint of Holland,
And Europe in the red religious stone:
All places in the room where we in love lie down.

A Dream Observed

Out from his bed the breaking seas
  By waking eyes unseen
Now fall, aquatic creatures whirl
  And he whirls through the ambient green.

The sea lion and the scolopendra
  Lolling in sleep he sees
Strange in their ways, and the swift changes
  Their landscape makes, from shells to trees.

Down English lanes a camel walks,
  Or untrammelled flies.
But I, wakeful and watching, see
  How chilly out of the clothes he lies.

Easy an act to cover him warm:
  Such a lover's small success
Like the heaped mind so humble in sleep
  But points our actual powerlessness.

Monsters in dreams he sees, yet lies
  At peace in his curling bed;
Blessings that outdo all distress
  Implicit in his sleeping head.

At Parting

Since we through war awhile must part
Sweetheart, and learn to lose
Daily use
Of all that satisfied our heart:
Lay up those secrets and those powers
Wherewith you pleased and cherished me these two years:

Now we must draw, as plants would,
On tubers stored in a better season,
Our honey and heaven;
Only our love can store such food.
Is this to make a god of absence?
A new-born monster to steal our sustenance?

We cannot quite cast out lack and pain.
Let him remain – what he may devour
We can well spare:
He never can tap this, the true vein.
I have no words to tell you what you were,
But when you are sad, think, Heaven could give no more.

For a Child Expected

Lovers whose lifted hands are candles in winter,
Whose gentle ways like streams in the easy summer,
Lying together
For secret setting of a child, love what they do,
Thinking they make that candle immortal, those streams
    forever flow,
And yet do better than they know.

So the first flutter of a baby felt in the womb,
Its little signal and promise of riches to come,
Is taken in its father's name;
Its life is the body of his love, like his caress,
First delicate and strange, that daily use
Makes dearer and priceless.

Our baby was to be the living sign of our joy,
Restore to each the other's lost infancy;
To a painter's pillaging eye
Poet's coiled hearing, add the heart we might earn
By the help of love; all that our passion would yield
We put to planning our child.

The world flowed in; whatever we liked we took:
For its hair, the gold curls of the November oak
We saw on our walk;
Snowberries that make a Milky Way in the wood
For its tender hands; calm screen of the frozen flood
For our care of its childhood.

But the birth of a child is an uncontrollable glory;
Cat's cradle of hopes will hold no living baby,
Long though it lay quietly.
And when our baby stirs and struggles to be born
It compels humility: what we began
Is now its own.

For *as the sun that shines through glass*
So Jesus in His Mother was.
Therefore every human creature,
Since it shares in His nature,
In candle-gold passion or white
Sharp star should show its own way of light.
May no parental dread or dream
Darken our darling's early beam:
May she grow to her right powers
Unperturbed by passion of ours.

Autumn Day

The raging colour of this cold Friday
Eats up our patience like a fire,
Consumes our willingness to endure.
Here the crumpled maple, a gold fabric,
The beech by beams empurpled, the holy sycamore,
Berries red-hot, the rose's core –
The sun emboldens to burn in porphyry and amber.

Pick up the remnants of our resignation
Where we left them, and bring our loving passion,
Before the mist from the dark sea at our feet
Where mushrooms cling like limpets in the grass,
Quenching our fierceness, leaves us in a worse case.

The Cranes

We thought they were gulls at first, while they were
   distant –
The two cranes flying out of a normal morning.
They circled twice about our house and sank,
Their long legs drooping, down over the wood.
We saw their wings flash white, frayed at the black tip,
And heard their harsh cry, like a rusty screw.
Down in the next field, shy and angular,
They darted their long necks in the grass for fish.
They would not have us close, but shambled coyly,
Ridiculous, caught on the ground. Yet our fields
Under their feet became a fen; the sky
That was blue July became watery November,
And echoing with the cries of foreign birds.

from *The Golden Bird* (1951)

Still Life

Night fell and the fog froze;
Six-pointed Venus first and then the moon rose.
Preparing granite against the morning
Fog was petrified; the moon shone, waiting.
The moon's light is visible silence:
In her quietness all is quiet, in suspense
Between the day and darkness a dubious brilliance
Every movement seems (unfocused) stealthy;
Rabbit across the lawn, stoat in the spinney,
On furtive errands. And within that light
There seems a presence waiting, just out of sight,
Holding its breath, waiting, the whole night.

Sleep, wake, sleep: it is there, just out of sight.

Night passed and the fog froze;
The moon passed, but not her silence: when the sun rose,
Rigid and mute his world, a fist
Clenched and contracted, every branch and plant encased
In quartz and scored with siliceous white –
A world struck solid and paralysed with light.

Absolute calm, absolute silence
Both to the eye and ear, but the skin feels violence,
Feels a pain whose origin is lost –
Impotent burning of the sun, or grip of the deaf-mute
    frost.

Dead and Gone

1

O that it were possible we might
But hold some two dayes conference with the dead
Duchess of Malfi

The coffin's typical shape
Implies for each a dear particular form:
The glory that was loved, caressed, endured,
Is carrion now, concealment but betrays it;
Hidden but known, lifeless but still the precious being.
Therefore, though each in pain is wholly alone,
The coffin is a common painful secret
Making of each an unwilling schizophrene:
For, what the imagination dares, the heart
Refuses; what the eye perceives, the heart
Knows to be falsehood; what the heart cries out
Receives an absolute negative from reason.

Then were all the other meetings traitors?
All those journeys when we flew and shone
Because toward each other, went toward this?
The perpetual hope, the hidden part of symbols,
Meant simply this: a sudden, public, death?
The dead could tell, but shares our longings no longer;
For once unfriendly, knows the whole or nothing
And shares nothing.   Yet we cannot part.
Till we confront his life with this his death
And make one sense of both, all thought's uncertain
All memory unsolved, and our condition
Changes from apathy to agony, either
Equally profitless.

For in the resurrection they neither marry, nor are
given in marriage

St Matthew's Gospel

The specialty of time and place
Were of love's making, and are gone;
From the unfocused blur of space
And the indifference of time
Struck by the force of joy and pain –
These will never come again.

True, the environment retains
A faithful passion: earth or stone,
Archway, tree or moving-stair –
The place cries out, cries out in pain:
Its cries are heard by you alone,
The moment will not come again.

So place is widowed. What remains?
Sayings and anniversaries,
Saints'-days that loss discovers,
Hagiography of lovers;
Worst, the gradual death of pain,
For the image will not come again.

And after such a loss, what gain?
Not the longed-for, that is certain.
Nothing, or else a new thing.
If there is any final meeting
It is past desire or pain.
If love is, love is to be born again.

He is dead and gone, Lady
Song

But O these dead, in dreams, in dreams returning.
So nearly true, they make awaking grief,
So far from true, that the true pain is relief.
Cruel, fickle, dissatisfied, sad,
Their life-like, life-betraying forms
Disquiet the night, disquiet the grave.
For it is we who haunt the dead
And not the dead haunt us – even
We tempt them, if their love constrains them
Still to will what we desire.

In dreams, in dreams returning. So we pursue them
With phantoms from a common past
Unexorcised. But lay these ghosts at last.
Why should Felicity long for us? Why should we wish it?
If death is double-faced, and turns
An opening look towards another world
That's out of sight. For present acquaintance, this:
The lids closed with cold coins,
The lips ajar, not for love
(This is neither enemy nor friend),
And yet for love to recognize the end.

Expectans Expectavi

The candid freezing season again:
Candle and cracker, needles of fir and frost;
Carols that through the night air pass, piercing
The glassy husk of heart and heaven;
Children's faces white in the pane, bright in the tree-light.

And the waiting season again,
That begs a crust and suffers joy vicariously:
In bodily starvation now, in the spirit's exile always.
O might the hilarious reign of love begin, let in
Like carols from the cold
The lost who crowd the pane, numb outcasts into
   welcome.

To Mark Time

For Benedict Ridler

To mark time is not to move:
Only the unkept hours drip from the clock
Or pull at the cord coiled in its groove,
The marker moveless, and the change illusion.

The sundial shows only delightful hours,
Nor seems to move although the shadow changes.
You who watch the moment, standing still
For the peace which, always coming, never will,

Look how this child marks time within his flesh
In multiplying cells whose life is movement;
Hold him in your arms and so enmesh
The moving moment, promise and fulfilment.

So nurse the joy of which the smiles speak;
See how his lashes, like the sundial's finger
Measuring only light – the heavenly light –
Mark this time in shadows on his cheek.

Piero della Francesca

The body is not fallen like the soul:
For these are godlike, being
Wholly of flesh, and in that being whole.
Founded on earth, they seem to be built not painted –
These huge girls, the mountain marble and
The valley clays were mixed for them,
The cleanness of lavender and the coolness of sand,
Also the tints of the deep sea;
And from the sea were made
The shell-like apse, and the pillars that echo each other
As waves do, in the Virgin's grey colonnade.

This gentle Jerome, with his Christ nailed
To the brown hill behind his head,
In speech with a stolid Donor, could not be
(Surely) by Manichaean doubts assailed;
In bodily peace this Solomon is wise:
Nothing is tortured, nothing ethereal here,
Nor would transcend the limits of material
Being, for in the flesh is nothing to fear
And nothing to despise.
The singing choir's not winged, for who would wish
To fly, whose feet may rest on earth?
Christ with his banner, Christ in Jordan's water,
Not humbled by his human birth.

Venetian Scene

(S. Giorgio Maggiore)

Fill the piazza with blue water
And gaze across domestic seas
From church to church. The tide is tame,
The streets look firm with floating marble.
Who made the sea ride in the city?
Movement is all a floating. Ride
The idle tide that smooths the steps:
Now statues ride in the blue air,
Light floats across the white façade
And seaweed over the marble stairs.

Backgrounds to Italian Paintings:
Fifteenth Century

Look between the bow and the bowstring, beneath
The flying feet of confederate angels,
Beyond old Montefeltro's triumph seat –
There the delectable landscape lies
Not furtive, but discreet:
It is not hiding, but withholds the secret.
What do the calm foreground figures know of it?
(Suffering martyrdom, riding a triumph
With a crowd of nymphs and Loves about the car)
What do they know of the scenes wherein they are?

The knees of the hills rise from wreaths of sleep,
The distant horsemen glimmer; the pigment fading
Has turned the juniper-green to brown;
And there the river winds away for ever.

We ourselves have walked those hills and valleys
Where the broom glows and the brittle rock-rose,
Combes are cool with chestnut and plains with poplar:
The juniper there was green – we have been
There, but were not given the secret,
Did not find our rest.

So give this land a stranger's look at best.

Later the landscape stole the picture, the human
Figures were banished, and with the figures vanished
From every natural scene the look of secrets.
So it seems that the figures held the clue.
Gaze at the story boldly as children do –

The wonder awaits you, cornerwise, but never
Full in the face; only the background promises,
Seen through the purple cones at the edge of the eye
And never to be understood:
The sleep-wreathed hills, the ever-winding river.

Deus Absconditus

. . . so shall we be drawn by that sight from Ignorance and
Sin . . . But by what cords? The cords of a man, and the cords
of Love.

Thomas Traherne

I selfish and forsaken do still long for you,
God for whom I was born and should have died:
Like lovers over miles and miles of sea
I lean my heart toward my comfort uselessly;
Did man or God weep out this sundering tide?

Cut off each sense, withdraw to the inmost secret place:
This God absconds from every promised land.
To shrink like a mollusc and to find no grace
This is the lot his lovers face.

And yet the worst is, not to seek you; yet the worst
Is not to know our lack of you. O, Love,
By what cords will you draw us? As at first
The cords of a man? Not splendour but the penal flesh
Taken for love, that moves us most.

Who breaks his tryst in a passionate ritual
May burn in a dry tree, a cold poem,
In the weak limbs of a child, so instant and perpetual,
In the stranger's face of a father dying,
Tender still but all the while departing.

Here he is endured, here he is adored.
And anywhere. Yet it is a long pursuit,
Carrying the junk and treasure of an ancient creed,
To a love who keeps his faith by seeming mute
And deaf, and dead indeed.

Blood Transfusion Centre

'He that gives, let him do it with simplicity.'

But which of us, waiting to offer his oblation
Can look at what he does with entire simplicity?
For between the lifeblood and the dying man
Science interposes its marvellous devices,
Isolating microbes, magnifying cells,
Testing, sealing, measuring, preserving.

So here we stand, in a queue for pure love
(Or it may be, for guilt, or it may be, for pride):
Shop-soiled housewives, typists and gardeners,
Lads and old soldiers – we look at each other
And wonder that health could spring from such
    complexions,
That such or such a man should design such a gift.
Yet each in his veins is offering the ichor,
Each has entertained the secret vision
Of health by his sickness; of life by his loss.

And here are the couches, with their patient figures
Whose blood is now flowing; and beyond these
The resting figures; and the cups of tea
Tasting of ether. The design is forgotten
In the details of performance: in chatting with the nurse,
In a sore vein, a thumping heart, a wearisome waiting.

To see this as godlike in the rest is to burden
The self who is one; to belittle it here
Belittles it in them. To give for those we love
Is natural as breathing, but should we not be hypocrites
To say that we loved this abstraction of Humanity?
The pelican's breast was not pierced for a stranger.
The man who gives his seed to beget for another
Creates he knows not what. The man who gives his blood
Restores he knows not what. We call in question
Such dangerous goodwill as moves in the first,
But what of the second? Who would have the right
To pretend to the impartial love of a god
And divide himself, not for a man but for Men?

Dindrane who gave her blood to succour a sick woman
And died so, did truly die another's death;
But the woman had her part – to live another's life,
And pain is as hard to relinquish as to bear.
So, toward a presence not abstract though not seen,
Both move, giver and receiver, through darkness.
(We speak of Love as blind, because his day is dark to us.)

The queue moves forward. Humbly we consider –
Humbly and with amazement –
'He that gives, let him do it with simplicity.'

The Constellation

Silent the Lyre that streams among the stars
And lulled is the fierce Lion:
So is Orpheus' torment turned
To memory and peace
Pricked out in stars a counterpoint that cannot sound.

So fixed, so quiet, the family constellations
Are memories of love or hate:
Yet each has had its hot creation
When with new sons the old forms fade
Before the calm irrevocable past is made.

These grow and sing: with their sweet jangling cries
The bickering soaring children
Elder with younger jostle for place.
Their milky light, their all-regarding gaze
Has travelled here a billion miles of space:
Distant they are, not fixed, nor frozen, nor at peace.

Mare Nostrum

Changeable beast with rumpled fur of foam
She plunges along the land,
Held by a moonstring, yet by solid rock
Hardly contained.

She is nothing to look at – only clouds and light
Contrive her vanishing jewels,
Her melting zircon and her solid agate.
If you would see her nature, watch

Those palpitating globes within the pool
More transparent yet more firm than mist:
Her life is a bubble of nothing, cool
Nothing, and like the jellyfish persists.

This yielding overpowers. All in her likeness
Are flutes and whorls in shell and rock and sand,
The conch full of her music,
The water-colours of wentletrap and fan.

And men who chose the shore, aeons ago,
Still spin their memories of her into glass,
Whose splinters worn by water seem to be
Solid green fragments of the sea.

But solid forms renounce her. As for men,
Though other vertebrates return,
Choice of dry land has lost her, let them swim
Each summer through her waves, they never find home.

The lost sea-nature. If her deeps are still,
She has given to men who yearn and may not return to
   them
Only the restless surface,
The quiet buried away,
The sunset shattered across the rocks in spray.

The Speech of the Dead

News of the dead is heard through words of the living.
After a casual phrase
Sometimes we burn with tears to recognize
Familiar words of the dead,
And Never again Never again cries against the loving
   greeting;
News of the dead, but by the living heard as
Dead news, and no true meeting.

No twittering ghosts, they speak as they always did,
But through our lips. Do they pursue and haunt us,
Or is it we who haunt them with the past, and will not rid
Their glory of that obsessive ghost?
O, in the sharp pale beams of the winter air
We seem to breathe their element, and the cold stir
About the brain is their interior speech.
They haunt us, and we them,
But it is our sad yearning that keeps them out of reach.

Those words out of the past that gave us pain
For the present, those are still our spirits' exchange,
But sounding through them now, most deeply felt,
A death- and a life-time's loss and gain.

The blind to each of their four senses add
A little skill and so atone for the fifth.
Might we, for that blind lack in not being dead,
Atone by greater silence and the skill

To guess and be still.
Not to imagine them sharing this or that
Our temporal activity, and turn
Their supernatural state to ours, but
To know them as they are through what we know they
    were;
And in that glory of love to learn
Words of the dead through living lips a prayer.

Michelangelo in the
Accademia (Florence)

Perfect in every part, the David
Reigns a heedless king of being:
All is said and all is freed.
But down the hall on either side
The prisoners strain toward existence:
They strain against the vice of stone
And agonise against the vice
Of shapelessness, and start the chain
Of atoms battering through the brain
To crack the clodding world apart.

And last of all the heavy Christ
Borne upward by his groaning creatures,
Bound within his death of stone,
That death in stone but partly done.
Undone for ever, yet the part
Strangely suffices, while we feel
The final truth in all our limbs
As growing outwards from the heart.

Villanelle for the Middle
of the Way

When we first love, his eyes reflect our own;
When mirrors change to windows we can see;
Seeing, we know how much is still unknown.

Was it a trite reflection? What is shown
When we gaze deep begins the mystery:
When we first love, his eyes reflect our own.

Neither of us could cast the first stone,
And to forgive is tender. 'Now', thought we,
'Seeing, we know.' How much was still unknown

We later learnt. But by forgiveness grown –
As Blake discovered – apt for eternity,
Though in first love his eyes reflect our own.

What was the crime for which you would atone
Or could be crime now between you and me
Seeing we know how much is still unknown?

I know you now by heart not eyes alone,
Dearer the dry than even the green tree.
When we first love, his eyes reflect our own,
Seeing, we know how much is still unknown.

from *The Golden Bird*

a poem based on Grimm's *Household Tale*

. . . So we came, in no measurable time,
To a place where three ways and two seasons meet –
In spring at the edge of Oxford.

'Here', said the Fox, 'is a city of screaming tyres,
Where lorries piled with motor-shells
Fly like clumsy maybugs through the streets,
And the river drumbles past exotic barges.
The smoke of learning rises with the river-mists,
And spires like funnels carry praise to heaven.
Thin and rare is the rising praise
But the heavenly thought descends in flesh and blood.
Once with tremendous wings vanning the sky
It seemed a flying horse, and prayed for, came
To kill the chimera of men's dismal fears;
Then sprang, like a diver rising from the depths, to
    Olympus,
Throwing its rider, who would have ridden to heaven
But had not learnt its horsemanship.
That speedy power feeds and drinks in this city:
Some have seen it here, but none has taken it.
Nor are you yet able to ride it:
Do not mount, but bring it by the bridle, softly.'

I crossed the bridge, with the whirling wrack of traffic.
The sky was laid below me in azure anemones,
The willows wept against the sun like rainbows
And punts as lazy as clouds slipped by beneath.
I came to the double gateway
Where the Stuarts guard the tranquil garden,

[37]

The chimes fall among rare plants like rain
And blackened ashlar walls debar
The rabble of 'prams and all disorderly persons'.
A wolf and boar of stone
Sat snarling back on their haunches,
And the Horse of the wind-outpacing thought
Quietly fed there, tasting
The luculent waxen blooms
Of the leafless magnolia tree.

I approached it softly:
Its mane was like the flowing stone
Of ripples on a Greek *stele*,
The sculptured waves of thought.
Its wings that could beat like waves were folded,
Its eyes the intuitive crystal, veiled,
Its phallus the power of creation, sleeping.
It turned and watched me calmly,
While I, on fire to master it
And once again forgetful,
Put my hand on its back, prepared to mount.
Whereat it lifted its head
And neighed to the top of Tom Tower.

On that, a white-haired man stepped out from the gate,
Who spoke to me – softly, but his words were cold
And more deadly than anger:
Of how one could not hope to master the truth
Without a lifetime's labour; even then
Only the few . . . and then I heard no more . . .

from *A Matter of Life and Death* (1959)

A Matter of Life and Death

I did not see the iris move,
I did not feel the unfurling of my love.

This was the sequence of the flower:
First the leaf from which the bud would swell,
No prison, but a cell,
A rolled rainbow;
Then the sheath that enclosed the blow
Pale and close
Giving no hint of the blaze within,
A tender skin with violet vein.
Then the first unfurling petal
As if a hand that held a jewel
Curled back a finger, let the light wink
Narrowly through the chink,
Or like the rays before the sunrise
Promising glory.

And while my back is turned, the flower has blown.
Impossible to tell
How this opulent blossom from that spick bud has grown.
The chrysalis curled tight,
The flower poised for flight –
Corolla with lolling porphyry wings
And yellow tiger markings
A chasing-place for shade and light:
Between these two, the explosion
Soundless, with no duration.
   (I did not see the iris move,
   I did not feel my love unfurl.)
The most tremendous change takes place in silence,
Unseen, however you mark the sequence,
Unheard, whatever the din of exploding stars.

[41]

Down the porphyry stair
Headlong into the air
The boy has come: he crouches there
A tender startled creature
With a fawn's ears and hair-spring poise
Alert to every danger
Aghast at every noise.
A blue blink
From under squeezed-up lids
As mauve as iris buds
Is gone as quickly as a bird's bright wink.
Gone – but as if his soul had looked an instant
    through the chink.
And perfect as his shell-like nails,
Close as are to the flower its petals,
My love unfolded with him.
Yet till this moment what was he to me?
Conjecture and analogy;
Conceived, and yet unknown;
Behind this narrow barrier of bone
Distant as any foreign land could be.

   I have seen the light of day,
   Was it sight or taste or smell?
   What I have been, who can tell?
   What I shall be, who can say?

He floats in life as a lily in the pool
Free and yet rooted;
And strong though seeming frail,
Like the ghost fritillary
That trails its first-appearing bud

As though too weak to raise it from the mud,
But is stronger than you dream,
And soon will lift its paper lantern
High upon an arched and sinewy stem.

His smiles are all largesse,
Need ask for no return,
Since give and take are meaningless
To one who gives by needing
And takes our love for granted
And grants a favour even by his greed.
The ballet of his twirling hands
His chirping and his loving sounds,
Perpetual expectation
Perpetual surprise –
Not a lifetime satisfies
For watching, every thing he does
We wish him to do always.

Only in a lover's eyes
Shall I be so approved again;
Only the other side of pain
Can truth again be all I speak,
Or I again possess
A saint's hilarious carelessness.

He rows about his ocean
With its leaning cliffs and towers,
A horizontal being,
Straddled by walking people
By table-legs and chairs;
And sees the world as you can see
Upside-down in water
The wavering heights of trees

Whose roots hang from your eyes.
Then Time begins to trail
In vanishing smoke behind him,
A vertical creature now
With a pocket full of nails,
One of a gang of urchin boys
Who proves his sex by robber noise –
Roar of the sucking dove
And thunder of the wren.
Terror waits in the woods
But in the sun he is brazen
Because our love is his
No matter what he does;
His very weakness claims a share
In the larger strength of others,
And perfect in our eyes
He is only vulnerable there.

But not immortal there, alas.
We cannot keep, and see. The shapes of clouds
Which alter as we gaze
Are not more transient than these living forms
Which we so long to hold
For ever in the moment's mould.
The figures frozen in the camera's record
And carried with us from the past
Are like those objects buried with the dead –
Temporal treasures irrelevant to their need.
Yes, this is the worst:
The living truth is lost,
And is supplanted by these album smiles.

What you desire to keep, you slay:
While you watch me, I am going.
Wiser than you, I would not stay
Even if I could: my hope's in growing.
My form as a dapple of sun that flies
On the brook, is changed; my earliest word
Is the call you learnt to recognize
And now forget, of a strange bird.

Yet, as the calyx contains the life of the bud
So the bud is contained within the flower
Though past in time:
The end is not more true than the beginning,
Nor is the promise cancelled by the prime.
Not only what he was, and is, but what he might have been,
In each is rolled within.
Our life depends on that:
What other claim have we to resurrection?
For now that we can contemplate perfection
We have lost the knack of being it. What should be saved
Of these distorted lives?

All we can pray is
                    Save us from Nothingness.
Nothingness, which all men dread;
Which makes us feel an irrational pity for the dead,
And fight the anodyne
Even while we long for deliverance from pain.

So, I have read,
When a man gave his darling in grief to the grave
About her neck in a locket tied
He set this urgent word –
Not to drink Lethe, at all costs not to forget.
And this is truth to us, even yet.

[45]

For if life is eternal
All must be held, though all must be redeemed.
But what can ever restore
To these sad and short-coming lives of ours
The lovely jocund creatures that we were
And did not know we were?
What can give us at once
The being and the sense?

Why, each within
Has kept his secret for some Resurrection:
The wonder that he was
And can be, which is his
Not by merit, only by grace.
It comes to light, as love is born with a child,
Neither with help nor herald
(I did not see the iris move);
Neither by sight nor sound –
I did not feel the unfurling of my love.

The Images that Hurt . . .

The images that hurt and that connect
W. H. Auden

All the materials of a poem
Are lying scattered about, as in this garden
The lovely lumber of Spring.
All is profusion, confusion: hundred-eyed
The primulae in crimson pink and purple,
Golden at the pupil;
Prodigal the nectarine and plum
That fret their petals against a rosy wall.
Flame of the tulip, fume of the blue anemone,
White Alps of blossom in the giant pear-tree,
Peaks and glaciers, rise from the same drab soil.

Far too much joy for comfort:
The images hurt because they won't connect.
No poem, no possession, therefore pain.
And struggling now to use
These images that bud from the bed of my mind
I grope about for a form,
As much in the dark, this white and dazzling day,
As the bulb at midwinter; as filled with longing
Even in this green garden
As those who gaze from the cliff at the depths of sea
And know they cannot possess it, being of the shore
And severed from that element for ever.

Choosing a Name

My little son, I have cast you out
  To hang heels upward, wailing over a world
  With walls too wide.
My faith till now, and now my love:
  No walls too wide for that to fill, no depth
  Too great for all you hide.

I love, not knowing what I love,
  I give, though ignorant for whom
  The history and power of a name.
I conjure with it, like a novice
  Summoning unknown spirits: answering me
  You take the word, and tame it.

Even as the gift of life
  You take the famous name you did not choose
  And make it new.
You and the name exchange a power:
  Its history is changed, becoming yours,
  And yours by this: who calls this, calls you.

Strong vessel of peace, and plenty promised,
  Into whose unsounded depths I pour
  This alien power;
Frail vessel, launched with a shawl for sail,
  Whose guiding spirit keeps his needle-quivering
  Poise between trust and terror,

And stares amazed to find himself alive;
  This is the means by which you say *I am*,
  Not to be lost till all is lost,
When at the sight of God you say *I am nothing*,
  And find, forgetting name and speech at last,
  A home not mine, dear outcast.

The Gaze

Your light is not yet broken:
Single the seven colours stream
In one white eyebeam from your self to mine.
My look, refracted and coloured by desires
Brings home a half-truth, but when you look at me
It is as though you had thrown a line
Out from your cradle to draw my image back.
Mirrors return the image which we show them,
But like a thinker, when you reflect on me
You take me in. And this without deceit,
Since you are open and since looks are free.

God is the source on which you should gaze like that.
I am not worth it; looking at me, you must learn
Selection, and suppress some part of the truth,
For art or kindness' sake. But not for love's.
For love (which has no need to blame or praise)
Waken that white beam again, reminding me
That I was born for this, to watch my Maker
Ever, with such a humble, thirsty gaze.

Nothing is Lost

Nothing is lost.
We are too sad to know that, or too blind;
Only in visited moments do we understand:
It is not that the dead return –
They are about us always, though unguessed.

This pencilled Latin verse
You dying wrote me, ten years past and more,
Brings you as much alive to me as the self you wrote it for,
Dear father, as I read your words
With no word but Alas.

Lines in a letter, lines in a face
Are faithful currents of life: the boy has written
His parents across his forehead, and as we burn
Our bodies up each seven years,
His own past self has left no plainer trace.

Nothing dies.
The cells pass on their secrets, we betray them
Unknowingly: in a freckle, in the way
We walk, recall some ancestor,
And Adam in the colour of our eyes.

Yes, on the face of the new born,
Before the soul has taken full possession,
There pass, as over a screen, in succession
The images of other beings:
Face after face looks out, and then is gone.

Nothing is lost, for all in love survive.
I lay my cheek against his sleeping limbs
To feel if he is warm, and touch in him
   Those children whom no shawl could warm,
      No arms, no grief, no longing could revive.

   Thus what we see, or know,
Is only a tiny portion, at the best,
Of the life in which we share; an iceberg's crest
   Our sunlit present, our partial sense,
      With deep supporting multitudes below.

Bathing off Roseland

The sea, that turns old bottles into gems,
  Has made of me a bird.
  Now with all four wings outspread
I dip and hover, vacillate, recover
    Lulled and directionless,
  Who on the cliff with conscious tread
    Moved to some purpose.

It is a firmament that curves below,
  Colour of capsicum green
  And purple bloom of aubergine;
Wayward and flippant I am in my element,
    Feeling the speed
  Of the wheeling world and the sails careening
    Above my head.

I am sustained by powers not my own,
  As on the tide of prayer
  Another's love can sway me toward
Some good that of myself I would not:
    Powerful, hidden to me,
  As the purpose which drives these great ships forward
    Parting the sea.

Lyme Regis – Golden Cap

For soul is form, and doth the body make
Spenser

The Cobb curves like a fossil, ridged and gray.
That sickle hook, which once held navies in its crook,
Still shields the town, and reaps the golden stalks
That spring in the wave;
Cliffs are sliced about the bay
Like Gloucester cheese (and the sea a bowl of pale whey);
These, and even the fossil shells
Uncovered by the tide twice in a day,
Immortal in clay their grave and their preservative,
Shall all be worn away.
That idling sauntering sea which suddenly shows its teeth
   in a white snarl,
That yielding seeling sea which hardly lifts a finger,
Steadily swallows the cliffs of clay
(And the spirit wears the flesh away):
The trembling hawk, the trembling sea, hard on their prey.

Rocks at the cliff's foot seem dead souls
Bound in these boulder shapes, with headless
Torsoes, rounded thighs and shoulders,
Bodies that would not take the mould
Of spirit, as though
The flesh for ever were only flesh:
Prone upon a forlorn shore
Until as small shingle all
Under the grinding tide are rolled.

Baptized of water and the spirit,
But not as rocks to shingle, not as cliffs to sand
Would we endure our transformation:
To move as light through water, not to be lost like a drop in
   the sea –
The body with the soul's design
Firm as the ammonite's, but free,
And by its form, divine.

Anniversary

This fig-tree spreads all hands toward the light,
   Five broad fingers to each, solid and still
   As those that are chiselled on pulpit or stall.
And yet the light pervades those carven leaves,
Not as my dark hands divert the sun
   If I hold them before my face –
   These invert it, let it pass,
A green effulgence that the trunk receives.

These fifteen years I have spread my hands to the light of
    your love.
Its rays should long ago have made me strong:
   Did my remorse for wrong
Or fears filter its power from the light,
Or did my darkness divert it from my heart,
   That I am still so callow and unsure,
   And cannot think to endure
Even the shortest winter out of your sight?

from *Some Time After* (1972)

For a New Voice

for George Fraser

Muse of middle-age, ice on the wings,
   Earthbound looks toward skies
Where once she looped and curtsied;
   Or, hovercraft close to the ground, goes
   On a cushion of stale air,
The breath of bygone verses.
Too conscious of too much, waits
   For the irresistible moment,
   Through days, months, years, silent.

Each year a bird moults, new plumes
   For old acquires, new voice
   After the winter whisper;
And a boy before his manhood comes
   Breaks his old flute, is given
   The key of bass or tenor.

O Muse, who should be heavenly, break
   My voice, make me a new one!
Rid me of this old sound-box,
   Trap of exhausted echoes
And coffin of past power.
   Make it anew, and now:
Not swan-like, in my dying hour
   Only to sing in pain,
   But now, a poet's voice again.

Corneal Graft

And after fifty years of blindness
The hand of science touched him, and he saw.

A face was a blur, poised on a stalk of speech;
Colour meant simply red; all planes were flat,
Except where memory, taught by his learnéd fingers,
Spoke to his 'prentice sight.
                              As for the moon,
The queen of heaven, she was a watery curd
Spilt on his window-pane,
For height, more than his stick could measure,
Was a senseless word.
The splendours of the morning gave no pleasure,
But he would rise at dawn to see
Distant cars and lorries, moving divinely
Across his strange horizon, stranger by far
Than the Pacific to the old explorers.

And is the patient grateful, subject of a miracle?

Blind, he was confident, forging through his twilight,
Heedless of dangers he had never seen.
As a dreamer on the brink of a ravine
Walks fearlessly, but waking, totters and falls,
So now the surging traffic appals him,
Monsters menace, he dare not cross:
A child, long past the childhood season;
A prince in darkness, but in the light a prisoner.

And if, after this five-sense living,
The hand of God should touch us to eternal light –
Not saints, well practised in that mode of seeing,
But grown-up babies, with a world to unlearn,
Menaced by marvels, how should we fare?
Dense, slow of response, only at the fingertips
Keeping some fragments of truth –
What could that heaven bring us but despair?

Mirror Image

When I look in the glass
    What creature looks back?
Not myself as I was,
    As I am, as I feel;
That face is not mine,
    Though reason declares
Soul and body are one.
    While my body was ageing
    What was I doing?
While cheeks grew hollow,
    While skin was coarsening,
    Eyelids drooping
    Where was I looking?

I looked at my friends
    And at you, my darling:
As a player who glances
Over his shoulder
    At Grandmother's Steps,
I knew you grown older
    Yet noticed no movement.
In you I engage
    The past and the present
In one bright image
    For ever true.

But while I watched *you*
  The girl in the mirror
Was making a face.
The self that I knew
  Is in focus no longer.
  'I want you to meet . . .'
My looking-glass says,
  And it shows me a stranger.

Thaw

The land takes breath; the iron grip
That clamped upon her heart is slackened.
On roofs the slithering snow-wrack
Like tods of sheep's wool slowly drips.

Earth's grey and foot-patched quilt of snow
Is wearing thin; the green shows through;
The carnival days of ice are gone,
The godlike skater's but a man.

As a sea-bird waddling on webbed feet
He is humbled; see him shamble
Clumsily up the hill, whose nimble
Swoops on the ice were a god in flight.

A curdled gravy chokes the gutters.
Yet on the lake the island glows
In crimson willow-twigs; the trees
Hold up the sky on bare, dark shoulders.

A Waving Hand

. . . the need to reconcile the fact of what has occurred with the
human imagination of it, to build up a sense of the past which is
also a sense of the present . . .

John Bayley on Pasternak and Tolstoy

The death that we shall die
Is here, we know, coiled like a spring inside us,
Waiting its time.
When what is now becomes the past, we can see its future
   implied
As seed in the fruit, child in the womb.
The gardener, stooping down to tie
His bootlace, died so,
And acts through a lifetime multiplied
Foreshadowed this: when as a boy
He learnt to tie a bow,
Or when he stooped each day to dibble his plants,
Something was meant, he could not know.

So men seem walking histories
Of their own futures: we look to see the design
Forward or backward, plain,
As rings in a tree-trunk tell the sequence of years.
The jilted boy in pain
Trudging the pavement under the heartless stars
Now with his darling joyfully walks the same street.
Old words, old phrases, fly homing into the future
Where the poem is complete.

Parting a week ago,
The baby waved, through tears. I waved back lightly
With no foreboding fears;

But I remember it now,
And scan and search the memory, as though it should
  explain
All that came after, the anguish of last night,
The ambulance dash, the kind indifferent nurses,
And now the cot, where she lies in a hospital gown
And waves to me, through tears.

Suppose, when we are dead,
The soul moves back, over the gulf of nescience,
To relive a lifetime, all that was done and said . . .
Some say remorse impels it, the pitiless conscience
That drives toward expiation;
But it might be a different need:
To live each *now* in the illumination
Of what's to come; wholly to understand
Those tears, that waving hand.

Winter Poem

November smells of rue, bitter and musky,
Of mould, and fungus, and fog at the blue dusk.
The Church repents, and the trees, scattering their riches,
Stand up in bare bones.
But already the green buds sharpen for the first spring day,
Red embers glow on the twigs of the pyrus japonica,
And clematis awns, those burnished curly wigs,
Feather for the seeds' flight.

Stark Advent songs, the busy fungus of decay –
They are works of darkness that prepare the light,
And soon the candid frost lays bare all secrets.

Too Much Skill

When the artless Doctor sees
No one hope, but of his Fees . . .
When his Potion and his Pill,
His, or none, or little skill
Meet for nothing but to kill,
    Sweet Spirit, comfort me.
                    Herrick: His Litanie

Weeping relations in a ring
    Round the Victorian death-bed stand:
A public, but a gracious ending,
    Custom-propped on either hand.

Death with the faithful butler waits
    Just farther off, until the soul
Nods an agreement to the Fates,
    Keeping a vestige of control,

The end accepted like the start.
    Yes, even howls and funeral pyre
Assign to Death his ritual part;
    Only our age must play the liar,

Forcing the worn-out heart to hop,
    The senile to renew his breath,
Deploying every skill, to reap
    A few poor months of life-in-death.

Grant me an artless doctor, Lord,
    Unapt with syringe, mask, or knife,
Who when my worn-out body's dead
    Will fail to bring me back to life.

Azalea in the House

This little shabby tree, forgotten all summer,
And crouched in its corner through December frost,
Now is brought indoors to keep its promise.
It speaks in a blaze, like a prophet returned from the
    wilderness:
The buds throw off their brown extinguishers, burst
Into flame, and March sees a midsummer feast.

Explosion of sunsets, archangels on a needle-point,
Red parliament of butterflies . . .
I cannot hold it with words, yet summer life
While winter howls out there behind the glass
And trees still clench their fists, must be too brief.

Scentless, infertile, kept from moth and rain,
Colour is its whole theme,
Like those vermilion rose-trees that bloom
In picture-books. They never drooped or faded,
But this has only a short month to shine,
And hours not spent in watching it are wasted.

A Taste for Truth

For *miracle*, they say, translate *a sign*.
If God made water into wine
What was his meaning? That his laws
Are not immutable? Though our state is miserable
Yet all might live in glory if they chose?
Wine of our joy and water of our tears
Are not so incompatible as we think
If the atoms did not change, but those who drank.

In salt water our life began
And our blood is a salt solution.
We live upon this one condition –
Salt is good, salt is bitter.
All men born have wept salt tears,
All have wished to run from pain
And yet to live; all might learn
To love the sharp maternal brine
Could salt water taste like wine.

And if we say that we were foreordained,
All that expense of stars was planned
To bring self-consciousness to birth –
Megalomania? Well, we share our earth
With cousins vile enough, clever enough
To make us humble as regards our skill.
And yet, if spiders abash man's pride of life,
They make his charity seem more marvellous still.

No cost of stars could seem too great
To have made man's love: love pays for all.
Harder to think it pays the debt
For man's pain, man's fall.
A woman bears a child, and sees
His doom (her gift) to suffer years
Of hopeless struggle with disease.
Another must endure the cries
Of hunger, with no crumb to give.
And here the radiant face of love
Perishes in a deadly radiance
At the hands of brother men
And the impartial brain of science.

The miracles of science are so often
Just what one would not wish; but then,
God's miracle of the universe
On any view seems worse.
That one should say 'All shall be well'
Is yet the strongest miracle of all.

The flesh that formed us can divide
To form a cancer, and the strength
That held our weakness be dissolved.
Even she, whose affable wit denied
The inordinate, when she came to die
Endured rebellion in her body.
I cannot forget her dreadful sickness,
Nor reconcile within my mind
Her cheerful life, her cruel end.
Yet in her dying eyes I saw
Bright pain and love inseparable,
Part of the truth and ineluctable.

Gide, who forswore belief in God,
Died like a hero, keen to know
The truth of death, and tell it somehow.
Honour to him who rejects nothing,
Peace to all memories! for we too
Would work that miracle if we could:
To taste the truth, and find it good.

New Poems

Free Fall

In the year 1900, a French tailor proposed
to fly from the top of the Eiffel Tower in
a robe he had himself devised and made.
Film cameras recorded the experiment.

A long while, a long long while it seems:
The bat-winged figure shaking his robe,
   The cameras purring.

It is Daedalus the tailor, up on the Eiffel Tower
Ready to fly. The year is 1900;
   We watch it, now.

. . . Shakes at his bat-robe, first to the right,
Then left, then right again, a twitch,
   A doubtful gesture.

'Cast thyself from the pinnacle, angels will bear thee up.'
So great a height – the wings will surely beat
   And bear me up?

Shaking his robe. A mile of film we are wasting:
Why doesn't he jump? In these long seconds
   What is he thinking?

That the plan was crazy, and the careful stitches
Shaped him a shroud? Perhaps he is wondering
   How to withdraw.

To pretend a flaw in the work, a change in the wind;
And imagines how it would be to face
   The jeering crowd,

[75]

Slink back to his trade and live, with nothing to live for.
So still he hesitates, and shakes his shroud,
   Then, suddenly, jumps.

Not even a flap from the wings. The lens below
Can barely follow the plummeting shape,
   So quick his fall,

Hollowing out his own grave.
We are caught between dismay and laughter
   Watching it now –

Not in a myth, not a century back, but now.
Ridiculous death. Yet as he stood on the tower,
   Shaking, shaking his robe,

He mimed what each man must in private try,
Poised on the parapet of darkness –
   Each in that crowd, and you, reader, and I.

Threescore and Ten

for N.N.

Praestet fides supplementum
Sensuum defectui

In every generation
The young acquire an image of their elders
Tranquil, assured, with every day mapped out
From punctual meals to reading by the fire.
Threescore and ten is not like that at all
We find on getting there. Life is not tranquil,
But someone else has come into the room
And looks at us from time to time.
                              To admit
He's there is one thing, but the trick is harder
To welcome and ignore him. For it seems
The old should live as though their days were endless,
Yet also, feeling the glance of death upon them
Think that all time is Now, waken the power
Which looks athwart our days to what's immortal,
The Third Eye, which sees where sense is dark.

Didyma: Apollo's Temple

Yes, the camera can lie –
Do not believe it, go there.
Crouch in the shade of a column
To escape the burning sun
And know yourself diminished.
Men are pygmies here, the breadth
And height defeat their stature.
Thus the god should tower
Above his worshippers, although
Their muscles and their skill
Heaved up the blocks and smoothed the vault
With perfect ashlar facing –
Those craftsman-slaves, who scored
Their lord's initials in the stone,
Token of payment owing.

'*Oui, on peut sauter*' calls the tourist
Taking a short cut. Not for me:
Imagination's not so bold.
I cannot roof the temple
Or make the pillars march
The huge rectangle once they held.

Just as it fell the column lies
With giant overlapping drums
And measures what is lost.
'*Ne peut pas sauter*,' but
Gliding out of an ageless past
The kestrels, chestnut-backed,
And hoodie-crows contest the air;

Stone spiders on the wall and living
Lizards above the sacred spring
Confuse the centuries.
It is enough that here
A man feels small and takes
An exeat from his daily self,
To breathe warm airs, and see
Within the sanctuary
The dragon-arum's purple spadix.

Red Square

Grim heads in a row
Above the mausoleum,
Enduring while the tanks roll by,
The world sees. The tourist,
Reckoning up the gilded domes
Under a cloudless sky
(All that investiture of light
On sprouting gourds of bright St Basil),
Bewildered, cannot marry
The evidence of what he knows
To the evidence of sight:
Shapes of a toy city,
The sun-washed, guilt-soaked, Kremlin.

Open House

Churches are best for prayer, that have least light
John Donne

But then, why build a church at all
Or dream of glory, when to crawl
Into a hole could serve us better?
Where each in a private mist and utter
Silence may tread the whorling path
To find God at his being's core.
And Grecian temples we admire
For lightness and lucidity
Roofed by the blue and sunny sky
In their true form were close and murky.

Alone, then, to the Alone —
Dark oracle, or bloody stone?
Cathedrals take another way:
Like plants, and phototropic, they
Spire toward heaven, learn from trees
The branching vault, and canopies
Of fretted space. The ecstasy
Of power is here, coiled like a spring,
A god's mysterious gaiety,
And peace that passes understanding.

And this is home to us, although
Our numbers break its calm, we pry
With flaccid curiosity
And stray about on weary feet.
We are not much to boast of, yet

Thinking of God men built this home
And signed the work with man's own name.
Bracing their word is, and austere,
Admonishing our weak despair:
'Renew all hope, who enter here.'

The Runaway

Barnard's Star, a faint red dwarf at a distance
(from Earth) of only 5.9 light-years . . . is not
moving steadily. It is weaving its way along,
and there can be no doubt that it is being
perturbed by an invisible companion.

from an article by Patrick Moore

Barnard's Star is coming towards us
At sixty-seven miles a second.
Five years the light by which we see him
Travelled to reach us. Barnard's Star
Is moving drunkenly, led astray
By an invisible companion.
His other name – The Runaway.

Runaway Star when Christ was born,
No visible light has crossed two thousand
Years of time to show you plain,
And every year you grow more distant.
Yet on a word we travel back
To meet that orbit,
And the hero of that story
Like an invisible companion
Deflects our course, perturbs our days.

High Bield, Little Langdale

for Delmar and Josephine

The stillness of that valley
To town-bred ears is positive as a sound.
At early light the tarn
On dark-green glass re-prints the slaty mountain,
And little grassy hills
With rounded slopes follow each other in canon.

If there is sound, it is sudden:
Flycatcher clacks, robin winds an alarm-clock,
Or flings his chain of silver notes
Out of the yew-tree; then in the distant quarry
A wheel screams, slicing at stone,
Where sombre Wetherlam shows his frown-marks
   eastward.

Bright image on the remembering eye,
Your mountains go with each of us departing,
And traverse England; so for me
A winter long they loom in summer plumage.

But you, with a remembering brush,
Live for them, set all seasons on your walls, your heart.

Infelix Dido

Ille dies primus leti primusque malorum
causa fuit . . . (Aen.IV.169)
(That day was the first of death and the first
cause of woes . . .)

In a cave, safe from the storm,
Dido coupled with her love.
Nymphs shrieked on the mountain-top,
Lightning flashed and earth sustained
The piercing javelins of rain.
'That was the day sorrow began.'

Virgil blamed her it seems, for love is the foe of decorum.
All her generous hospitality counts for nothing:
Welcome given to beggars, the shipwrecked penniless
   Trojans,
Shelter provided, a share in the kingdom, while their
   leader
Prays the gods to reward her, if justice rules in heaven;
Prays that she may be blessed as she is prodigal in
   blessing.

'How could I help but fall in love?
Bursting from the cloud your beauty
Seized my heart, your history
Melted all my soul in pity.
Why could not your destiny
March to one end with my desire?'

[85]

That is all irrelevant, the poem seems to be saying:
Things are as they are; the order of heavenly justice
Takes no account of the debt he owed, of pity or anguish,
Pays no heed to the irony when Aeneas asks a blessing.
She was entrapped by a god? So much the worse for her.

  'Was not ours a marriage bed?
  Jewelled sword I gave you, purple
  Cloak you wore for me – my passion
  Woke an answering fire in you.
  Winter-long that torch was burning:
  How could you say it was no marriage?
  How could you say you gave no pledge?

  'For such a wound there's no forgiveness.
  Though you declare your heart is wracked
  You yield too swiftly, follow your fate
  Too willingly. My only solace
  Since my desire is turned to hate
  Is that in dying I can curse.'

Fame and success for him, who obeyed with such alacrity,
And dared not tell her the news, but let her heart divine it.
Death in despair for her, and the epithet *unlucky*.
Yes, but the poem brought revenge, for Virgil's genius –
Whether he knew it or not – pronounced in Dido's favour:
Type of all tender hearts deceived, of prodigal givers
More loving than belov'd, and by their love betrayed.

Night Watches

Somnus lies on a couch of feathers,
Curtains, black, around his head
And dreams beside him. Breathing quietly
Lie the lucky who share his bed.

They in a moment cover the hours
From night to morning; but the rest
Deep in the gulf must feel their way
From hour to hour, with lids shut tight
On anxious eyes, groping alone
Toward a distant thought of light.

Friendly Somnus, show me the gate
Youth took for granted; now I am old
Let me not count those endless hours
Till time is short again, and day
Recalls with half-incredulous pain
The caverns of such a long, long night.

Requiem

for R.C.B. 1905–83

Lichen coats the pear-tree bark,
  Sap must still make shift to rise.
Under skin a touch will bruise
Blood commutes in ceaseless journeys;
  Occult word that gives release
    Never conscious mind has spoken.

The animal is fain to die,
  The soul prepares an end, but still
  A hidden tyrant thwarts the will.
Yet he must yield, we know, though none
  Returns to share the secret, tell
    How at the last his power was broken.

Patient face upon the pillow
  We have seen our last of you,
Yet have not taken leave; we find
  Loss brings the subject closer, as
    The telephoto lens
  Distorts perspective, images
From far ago crowd on the mind.

You rise immortal there, although
  The curtains slide across and hide
The bier that bears you to the fire.
  A boy, a man, behind the eyes
    Of every grieving face
  Freely moves with a frolic life,
Multifarious, debonair.

It wakes our longing, brings no comfort,
   Yet with a kind of joy attests
We loved no phantom. All will see
   The jaunty beret, quizzical smile.
     I add an impatient candid boy
   Who seven years before me climbed
To the platform in the cedar tree.

But later days' humiliation,
   Helplessness of once-proud flesh,
Tormenting clamour in the brain –
   These I would forget, dear brother.
     Yet through them I perceive
   The shining of your valiant patience.
So, dark outlines, they remain.

Song to Mark a Boundary

for the Blands at Augop

In these tall trees warbler and wren all day
Beat boundaries of music, marking a province.
The song of birds is functional, they say:
This year at least its function is delight
For you in a new-built house, here tasting a first May.
The notes seem colour of spring made into sound:
Viridian leaves of beech, and powdery gay
Yellow of hornbeam, all that your window sees;
Green slopes and golden kingcups for the play
Of evening light, where the obedient trees
Compose a parkland picture; far away
The hills of Radnor Forest – I name them yours,
For the eye possesses what it can survey.

New come, and well come now to the birds' kingdom
This mortal nest – newcomer but no rival.
My poem too is functional: I sing
To claim your territory, and to pray
A blessing on your house, and on your stay.

Immigrants

The Scandinavian *corps de ballet*
Usurps the lawn.
Twists and turns display an elegant
Slate-gray back; in speckled brown
And slashed with scarlet, smaller rivals
Move into place.
Sallying and retreating trace
An intricate figure in the snow.
The fixed points are fallen apples,
Hunger the choreographer.

Flutter and squabble disturb the surface.
All at once
Fieldfares abandoning the contest
Fill the trees like winter fruit.
A solitary mistle thrush
Arrives to scour the empty skins;
Redwings brood
As though the snow were a warm nest.

Cruel winter, friendly to me,
Accept my thanks.
Starvation and the snow combine
To bring me glory:
Watching the visitants, I exult
And think them mine.

Bempton Cliffs

Strangely quiet, the cliffs are, as we approach.
The sea swallows the sound until, suddenly,
As though a door were opened into a hall
(A prayer meeting, a gaggle of gossiping talkers)
It's there, around us. And the sky in shreds
With whirling birds.

Now I am earthbound in a city of fliers,
A rooted maypole, while about my head
The dancers weave their patterns, maypole ribbons
Of varying flight, and their incessant cries
Are skeins of sound, flung up into the air.

Law rules the dance; in all these comings and goings
None is aimless. And all comparisons –
Comic, anthropomorphic – that spring to mind
At the sight of guillemots, tier upon tier
In dinner-jackets, like a festival chorus,
Are out of place.
                    Comparisons anyhow
Die in astonishment when we reach the cliff
Where the great ocean birds are perched.

That was no tractor you heard, but the gannets' talk.

The gale-masters, precipitous plungers,
Brood here on their scraps of net
With smaller birds around them, Viking beak
With its armoured look, subdued for a mating kiss,
Domestic as a farmyard goose;
So close, it seems as though a hand stretched out
Could touch and stroke the saffron head.

Jynx Torquilla

A Spell in the Air

In sallow winter days I remember
Jynx, jynx, the wryneck's call.

Not as the cuckoo's mate, but an August passenger
Blown off course, perhaps,
It stopped by, the husbandman's reward
For leaving ants about in the garden.

Its head, as though on stretched elastic,
Wobbled slightly as it flew
(The neck, they say, writhes like a snake in courting).
Its plumage, colour of gnarled bark
Speckled with lichen,
And sticky tongue, lethal to ants,
Were ours to watch, while the feast lasted;
Then it took off, for Africa.

Jynx, jynx, I heard you cry.
For this, witches would catch and bind you on a wheel
To draw the souls of men on invisible threads,
And turning, screeching, with your spell –
Jynx, jynx –
Recapture faithless lovers.

Azizur

*(A ten-year-old Bangladeshi boy, whose
mother was learning English from me.)*

Brown boy, quicksilver glance, dark thatch of hair,
Orphaned of the warm Ganges,
Adopted son of our chilly white-willowy Thames,
Where can we meet, except in the Tower of Babel,
What pleasures can we share?

My life, my likings, are unresonant to you
As dolphin-talk to human ear,
And yours to me are not much clearer.
I must discard the image of my sons, while
Well-brushed, sedate, with an orange tie,
In Blenheim Park you plod politely by me,
Smiling, but tired in a half mile.

You are your parents' word-winner,
Earning for them the precious coinage of speech.
You guide your mother's finger over her primer,
A fragile bridge between
The bright voluble India of home
And the world where she is dumb.

Smiles, plentiful smiles we share,
And the wish to give, and the sunny taste of a mango.

Wentworth Place: Keats Grove

The setting sun will always set me to rights . . .
Keats, to Benjamin Bailey

Keats fancied that the nightingale was happy
Because it sang. So beautiful his garden,
Behind the gate that shuts the present out
With all its greed and grimy noise,
I fall into a like mistake, to think –
Because there are such depths of peace and greenness,
Greenness and peace, because the mulberry
Invites with arms supported like the prophet,
Because the chestnut candles glimmer crimson –
That heartache could not flourish among these flowers,
Nor anguish resist the whisper of the leaves.

Angry for him, blessing his gift, I accuse
The paradise that could not save him,
Sickness and grief that sunsets could not heal.

Charles Williams: In Anamnesis

'That which was once Taliessin
rides to the barrows of Wales'

This is a likeness but it does not speak.
  The words are echoes, the image looks from the wall
Of many minds, kindling in each the spark
  Of passionate joy, yet silent in them all.
Pupils grow older, but a long-dead master
  Stands where they parted, ageless on his hill.
The child grows to be father of his father,
  Yet keeps relation, kneels in homage still.

What is the speech of the dead? Words on a page
  Where Taliessin launched his lines of glory
  Capture for him a poet's immortality
As every reader wakes them. So the image
  Speaks through a living mind, as he in life
  Would use from each the little that each could give.

The Halcyons

How Ceyx, son of Lucifer, and his wife Alcyone,*
daughter of Aeolus, were changed into birds
Ovid, Metamorphosis XI

1

Gently the waves
    On winter seas
Dandle the nest
    Through the calm solstice.

While storms menace
    A smooth dark space
Opens on furrows
    That dip and arise.

But by what sorrows
    Such peace was won
Is the bird's secret,
    The bright halcyon.

*I pronounce it to rhyme with 'Hermione'.

2

'Not over the sea, my love, do not set sail over sea,
For the winds are pitiless; I heard them in my childhood
Howling through my father's caves. If you must go
Let the journey be over land.' So Alcyone begged,
But gentle Ceyx, son of the morning star, would not listen,
Dearly though he loved her: disasters and portents,
A brother's fearful fate, robbed him of his rest:
He must consult the oracle, peregrine over seas
To understand the meaning, discover the remedy.
'At least take me with you, or I shall believe
I am dearer to you absent,' Alcyone said smiling.
'It is the loss of you, not suffering, I fear.
All is joy, if shared with you.'
                              'Then send your heart with me,
And keep your body, that I worship, safe for me on land.
I swear I shall return.'
                              Foreboding on the shore
She waves goodbye. The oars are double-banked, the
    hoisted sail
Soon drops below the horizon. Then begin the counted
    hours,
The empty days; the only solace picturing
His dear return, his arms around her – that and a faithful
    prayer
Each day to Juno; incense burnt, and candles lit.
But while she prays, a storm has caught his ship;
    mountainous waves
Crash on the deck, the mast is gone, oars and rudder
    smashed,
The captain's frantic shout unheard in the howling of the
    wind.

The ship shudders: now a hulk she lifts to a dizzy height
Then plunges sideways; all are lost in the writhing boiling
    water,
And Ceyx in the sea's throat calls out your name, Alcyone.

Even the pagan gods are not so heartless as we think them:
Hopeful prayers, where no hope can be, disturb the
    Olympian peace.
So, that Alcyone may know the truth in a true dream,
Juno summons from the cave of dreams Morpheus the son
    of Sleep
Who can assume all human forms.
                              Into her sleep he came
As from the sea, the water streaming from his hair and
    beard.
He seemed alive, as visions do, and yet she knew him
    dead.
'Precious Alcyone, your tears are all you owe me now,
For I am drowned. Your prayers could not turn aside the
    storm
Nor pacify the hungry seas. While I could I called your
    name
Until the waters closed over my head.'
                              She sprang to clasp him –
Poor naked ghost – embraced the air, and crying 'Take me
    with you,
I cannot live,' ran to the shore, as though the sea that stole
    him
Might hold him still . . .
                    So far the story might be yours or mine:
Parting, death, and a revenant in dream; but this is fable,
And winged beyond our common skill to master fate.

As dawn broke she gazed over the dreary rolling waters
And saw far out a shape – was it a boat, was it a corpse?
Nearer and nearer it came, and as a wave lifted it high
She knew her husband's face, and knew that he fulfilled
His promise to return. At once, frantic to reach him
She ran to the little jetty, leapt, flew into the sea.

Changing as she flew, she uttered harsh sounds,
And reached him, a bird. The kisses of that bird's beak
Renewed his spark of life; intensity of longing
Drew him alive to share her nature.

                              So the life they share
Is not the life they lost, yet, always together
They mate and rear their young. In the winter solstice
Her father Aeolus locks up the winds;
While she broods, men call it the kingfisher weather.

3

When misery is greatest
  Souls take wing,
Feathered by desire
  Or despair, rejecting
Intolerable fact,
  Take flight into madness
Or die by their own act.

Away into the sky
  From the squalor of Milan
The luckless children fly
  In de Sica's film,
  As though to affirm
That there is no solution
  For life's cruelty,
  Only to fly away.

But something more is meant
  By those myths of bird-changes.
That love continues blest
  In different guises;
That immortality
  Is not mere repetition:
It is a blue flash,
  A kingfisher vision.
It is a new-feathered
  And procreant love,
Seen where the halcyon
  Nests on the wave.